Great Zoos of the United States
Saint Louis Zoo

Janet Powell

The Rosen Publishing Group's
PowerKids Press™
New York

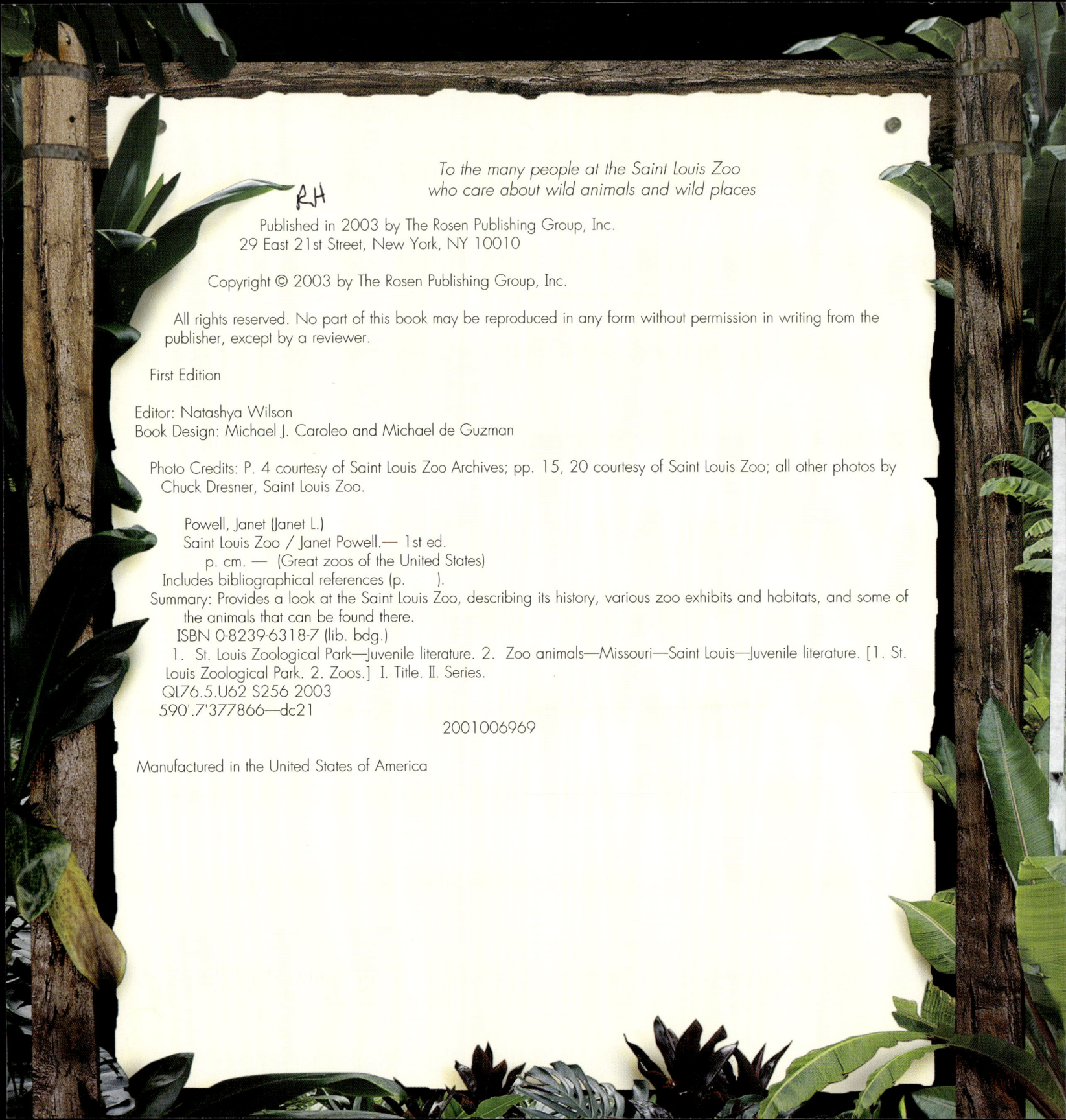

*To the many people at the Saint Louis Zoo
who care about wild animals and wild places*

Published in 2003 by The Rosen Publishing Group, Inc.
29 East 21st Street, New York, NY 10010

Copyright © 2003 by The Rosen Publishing Group, Inc.

All rights reserved. No part of this book may be reproduced in any form without permission in writing from the publisher, except by a reviewer.

First Edition

Editor: Natashya Wilson
Book Design: Michael J. Caroleo and Michael de Guzman

Photo Credits: P. 4 courtesy of Saint Louis Zoo Archives; pp. 15, 20 courtesy of Saint Louis Zoo; all other photos by Chuck Dresner, Saint Louis Zoo.

Powell, Janet (Janet L.)
Saint Louis Zoo / Janet Powell.— 1st ed.
   p. cm. — (Great zoos of the United States)
Includes bibliographical references (p.   ).
Summary: Provides a look at the Saint Louis Zoo, describing its history, various zoo exhibits and habitats, and some of the animals that can be found there.
   ISBN 0-8239-6318-7 (lib. bdg.)
  1. St. Louis Zoological Park—Juvenile literature. 2. Zoo animals—Missouri—Saint Louis—Juvenile literature. [1. St. Louis Zoological Park. 2. Zoos.] I. Title. II. Series.
QL76.5.U62 S256 2003
590'.7'377866—dc21
                                                            2001006969

Manufactured in the United States of America

Contents

1	A Walk in the Park	5
2	Our Town	6
3	Time to Play	9
4	River's Edge	10
5	Raja	13
6	Let's Pretend	14
7	Going Buggy at the Zoo	17
8	Baby Animals	18
9	A Helping Hand	21
10	Beyond the Zoo	22
	Glossary	23
	Index	24
	Web Sites	24

This photo of the birdcage was taken in the early 1900s. The cage is 228 feet (69 m) long, 84 feet (26 m) wide, and 50 feet (15 m) high.

A Walk in the Park

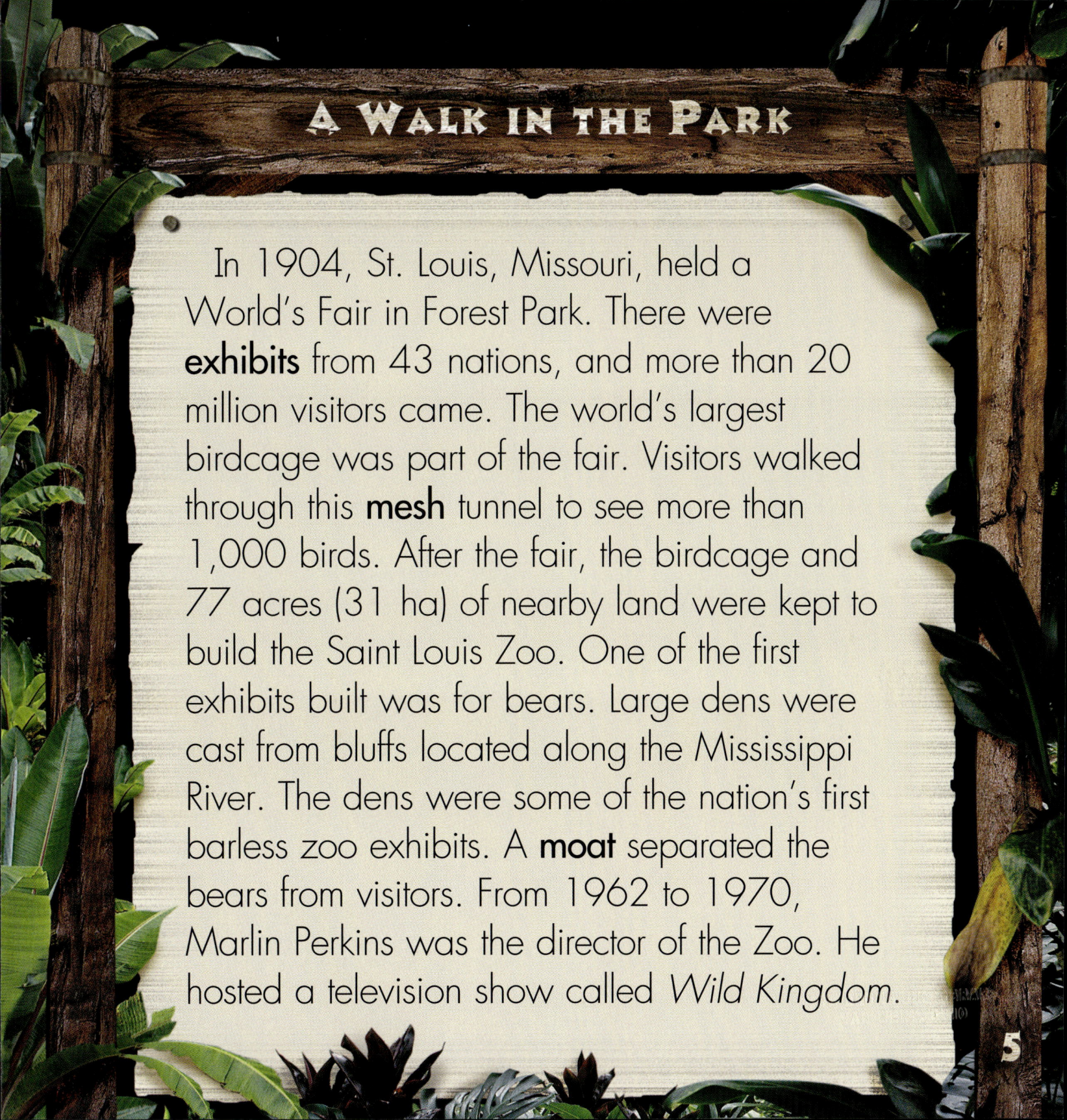

In 1904, St. Louis, Missouri, held a World's Fair in Forest Park. There were **exhibits** from 43 nations, and more than 20 million visitors came. The world's largest birdcage was part of the fair. Visitors walked through this **mesh** tunnel to see more than 1,000 birds. After the fair, the birdcage and 77 acres (31 ha) of nearby land were kept to build the Saint Louis Zoo. One of the first exhibits built was for bears. Large dens were cast from bluffs located along the Mississippi River. The dens were some of the nation's first barless zoo exhibits. A **moat** separated the bears from visitors. From 1962 to 1970, Marlin Perkins was the director of the Zoo. He hosted a television show called *Wild Kingdom*.

Our Town

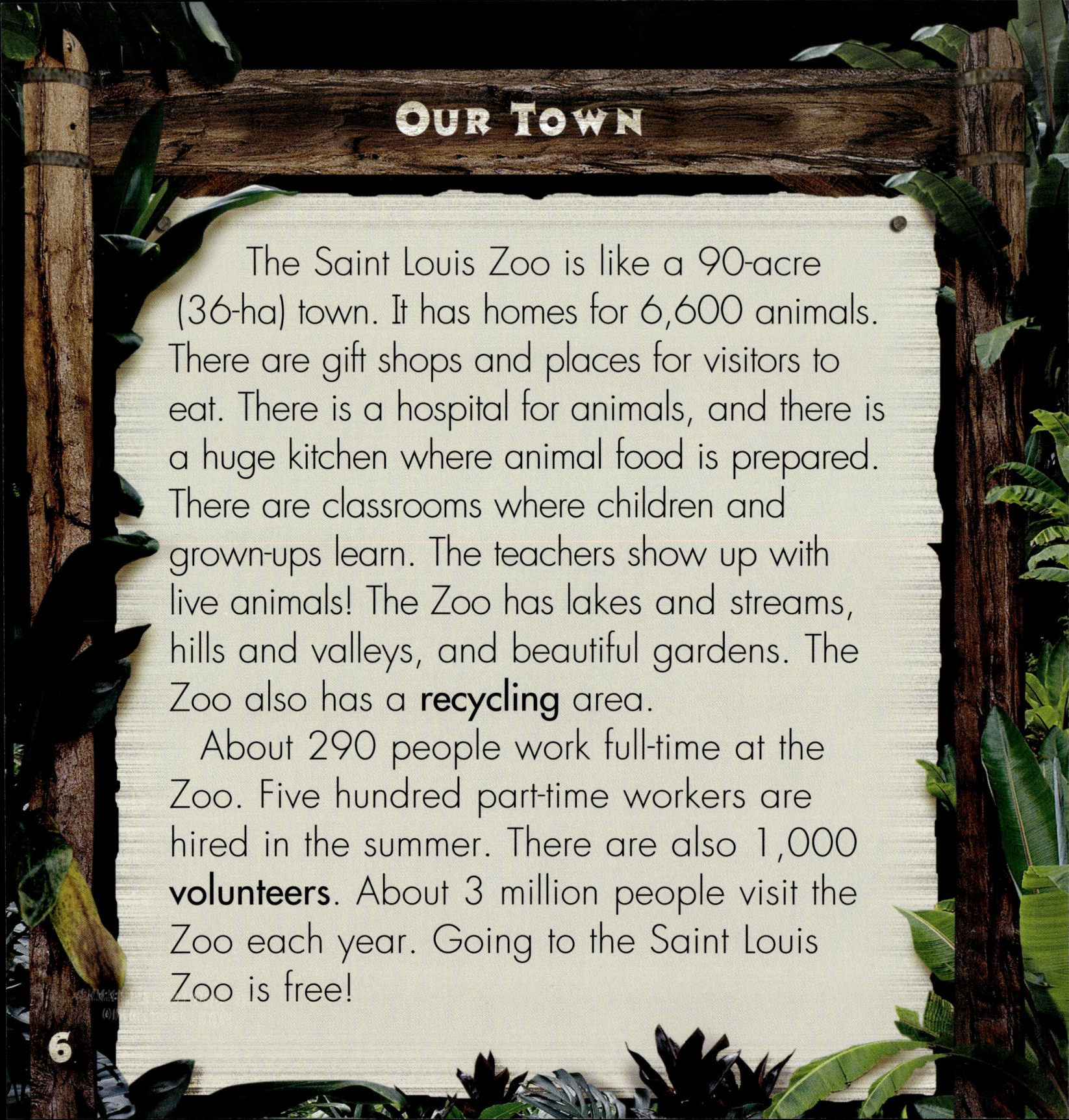

The Saint Louis Zoo is like a 90-acre (36-ha) town. It has homes for 6,600 animals. There are gift shops and places for visitors to eat. There is a hospital for animals, and there is a huge kitchen where animal food is prepared. There are classrooms where children and grown-ups learn. The teachers show up with live animals! The Zoo has lakes and streams, hills and valleys, and beautiful gardens. The Zoo also has a **recycling** area.

About 290 people work full-time at the Zoo. Five hundred part-time workers are hired in the summer. There are also 1,000 **volunteers**. About 3 million people visit the Zoo each year. Going to the Saint Louis Zoo is free!

A map is handed out to each visitor to guide him or her around the Zoo. Drawings show where each type of animal lives.

Visitors can ride a train to get around the Zoo. There are four train stops where they can get on and off.

DID YOU KNOW?

The tongue of a lorikeet, a colorful, little parrot, is shaped like a brush to lap up nectar.

Lorikeets will land on children's hands, shoulders, and even on their heads.

Children can pretend to be spiders as they climb around on a giant web made of rope.

One meerkat stands guard at the top of a termite mound while other meerkats search for food.

Kids can pop up in the Frog Surround to see colorful poison dart frogs.

Time to Play

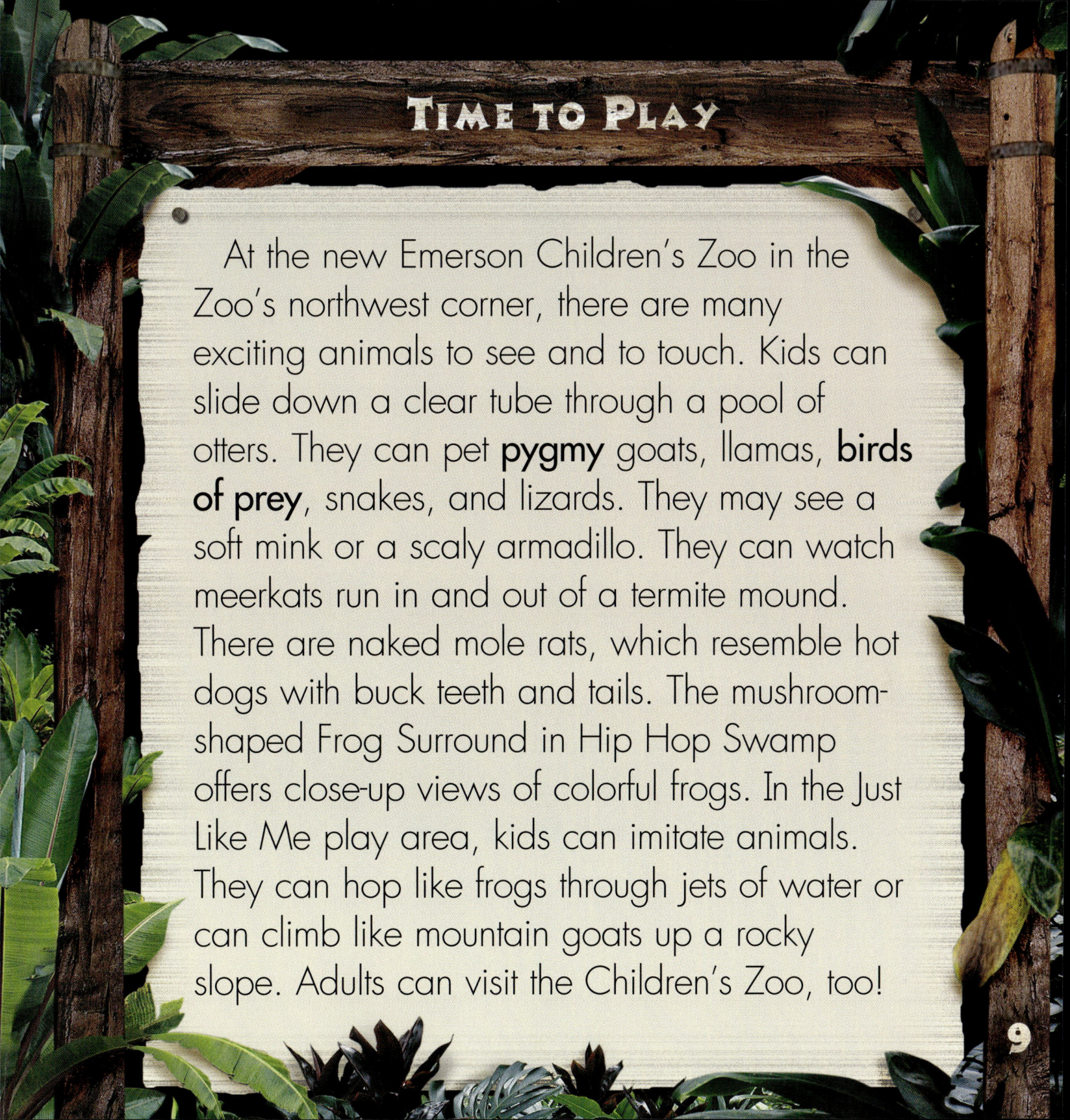

At the new Emerson Children's Zoo in the Zoo's northwest corner, there are many exciting animals to see and to touch. Kids can slide down a clear tube through a pool of otters. They can pet **pygmy** goats, llamas, **birds of prey**, snakes, and lizards. They may see a soft mink or a scaly armadillo. They can watch meerkats run in and out of a termite mound. There are naked mole rats, which resemble hot dogs with buck teeth and tails. The mushroom-shaped Frog Surround in Hip Hop Swamp offers close-up views of colorful frogs. In the Just Like Me play area, kids can imitate animals. They can hop like frogs through jets of water or can climb like mountain goats up a rocky slope. Adults can visit the Children's Zoo, too!

River's Edge

South of the Children's Zoo is a new exhibit called River's Edge. As visitors enter, waterfalls splash into a river that runs beside the path. The barriers between people and animals are hidden in trees and bushes. Birds chirp and monkeys chatter overhead. Visitors will see animals from South America, including **capybaras** and giant anteaters. African animals are farther down the path. There are warthogs, black rhinos, and hyenas. Hippos can be seen swimming underwater. They sometimes climb out onto land. Asian elephants are around the bend. At the end, visitors can explore the Missouri **wetlands** display. Many animals live in wetland **habitats**. This display explains why we must protect the wetlands.

At River's Edge, an Asian elephant is just one of the many types of animals that live among the trees and the flowering bushes.

There are not many Asian elephants left in the world. The Zoo hopes that someday Raja will have a family of his own.

RAJA

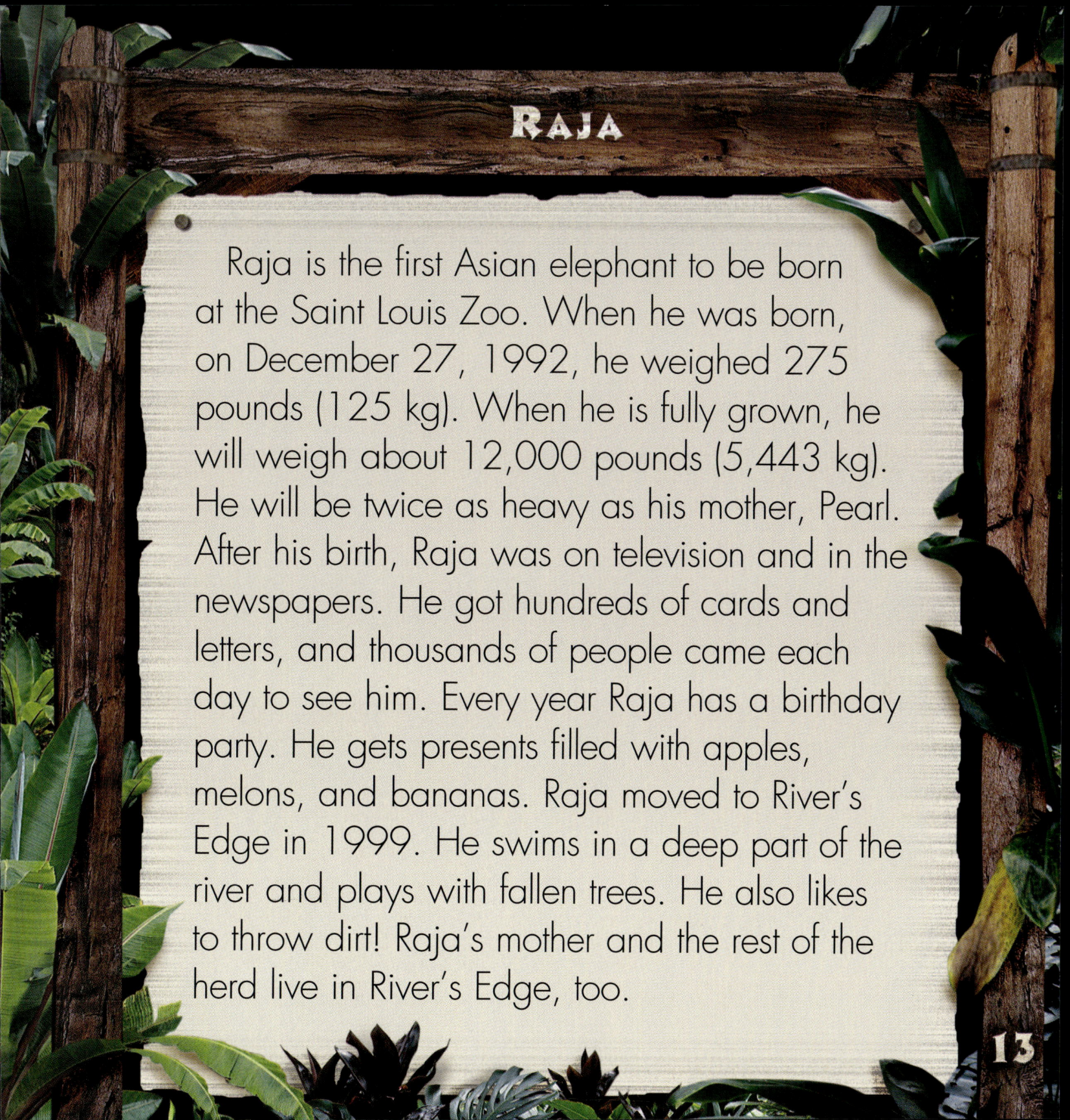

Raja is the first Asian elephant to be born at the Saint Louis Zoo. When he was born, on December 27, 1992, he weighed 275 pounds (125 kg). When he is fully grown, he will weigh about 12,000 pounds (5,443 kg). He will be twice as heavy as his mother, Pearl. After his birth, Raja was on television and in the newspapers. He got hundreds of cards and letters, and thousands of people came each day to see him. Every year Raja has a birthday party. He gets presents filled with apples, melons, and bananas. Raja moved to River's Edge in 1999. He swims in a deep part of the river and plays with fallen trees. He also likes to throw dirt! Raja's mother and the rest of the herd live in River's Edge, too.

Let's Pretend

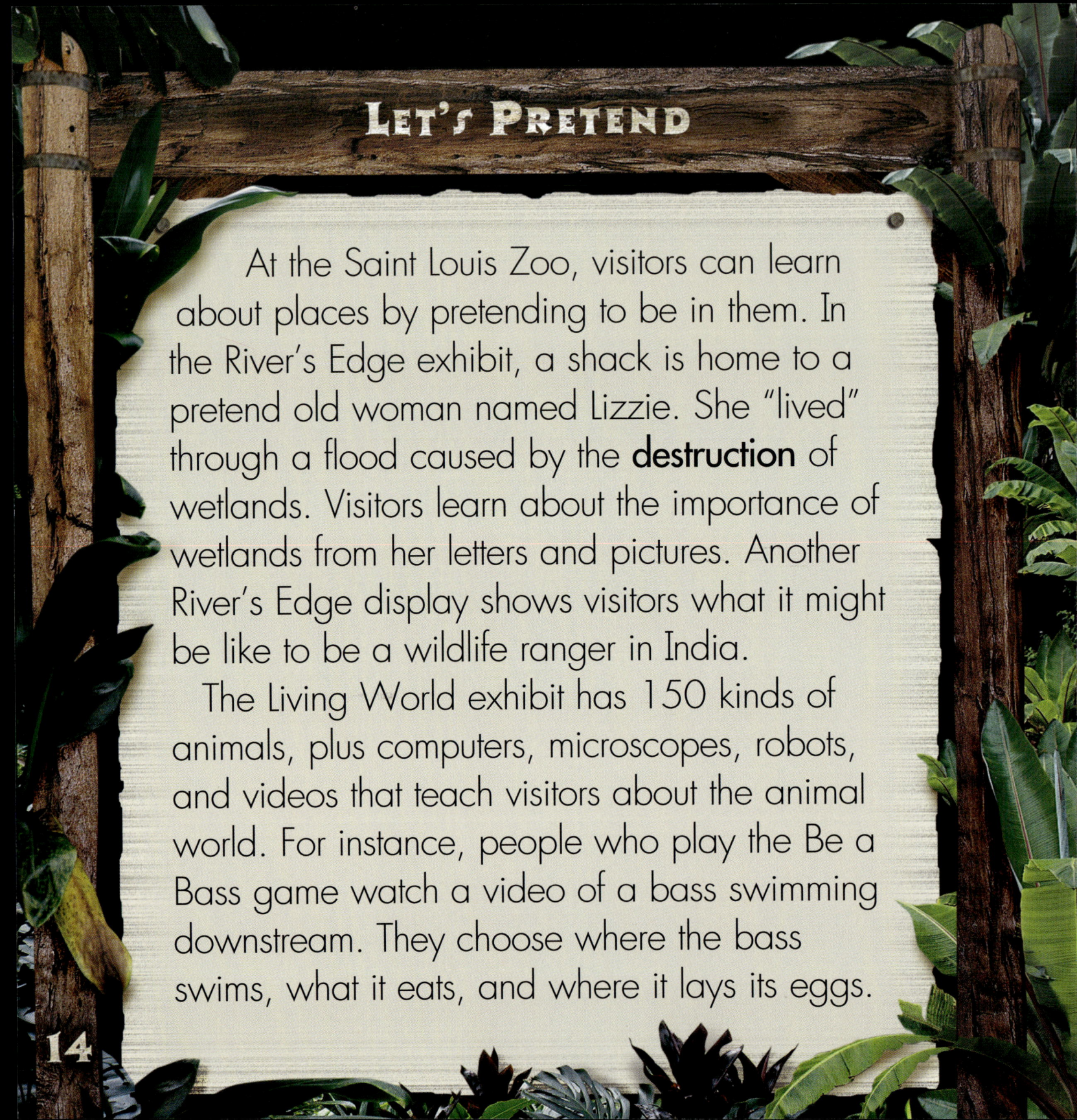

At the Saint Louis Zoo, visitors can learn about places by pretending to be in them. In the River's Edge exhibit, a shack is home to a pretend old woman named Lizzie. She "lived" through a flood caused by the **destruction** of wetlands. Visitors learn about the importance of wetlands from her letters and pictures. Another River's Edge display shows visitors what it might be like to be a wildlife ranger in India.

The Living World exhibit has 150 kinds of animals, plus computers, microscopes, robots, and videos that teach visitors about the animal world. For instance, people who play the Be a Bass game watch a video of a bass swimming downstream. They choose where the bass swims, what it eats, and where it lays its eggs.

This is Lizzie's shack. Visitors who see her letters and photos will learn why saving wetlands helps to prevent floods.

15

The Insectarium houses beetles and grasshoppers, and has a butterfly dome with 30 different kinds of butterflies and moths.

Going Buggy at the Zoo

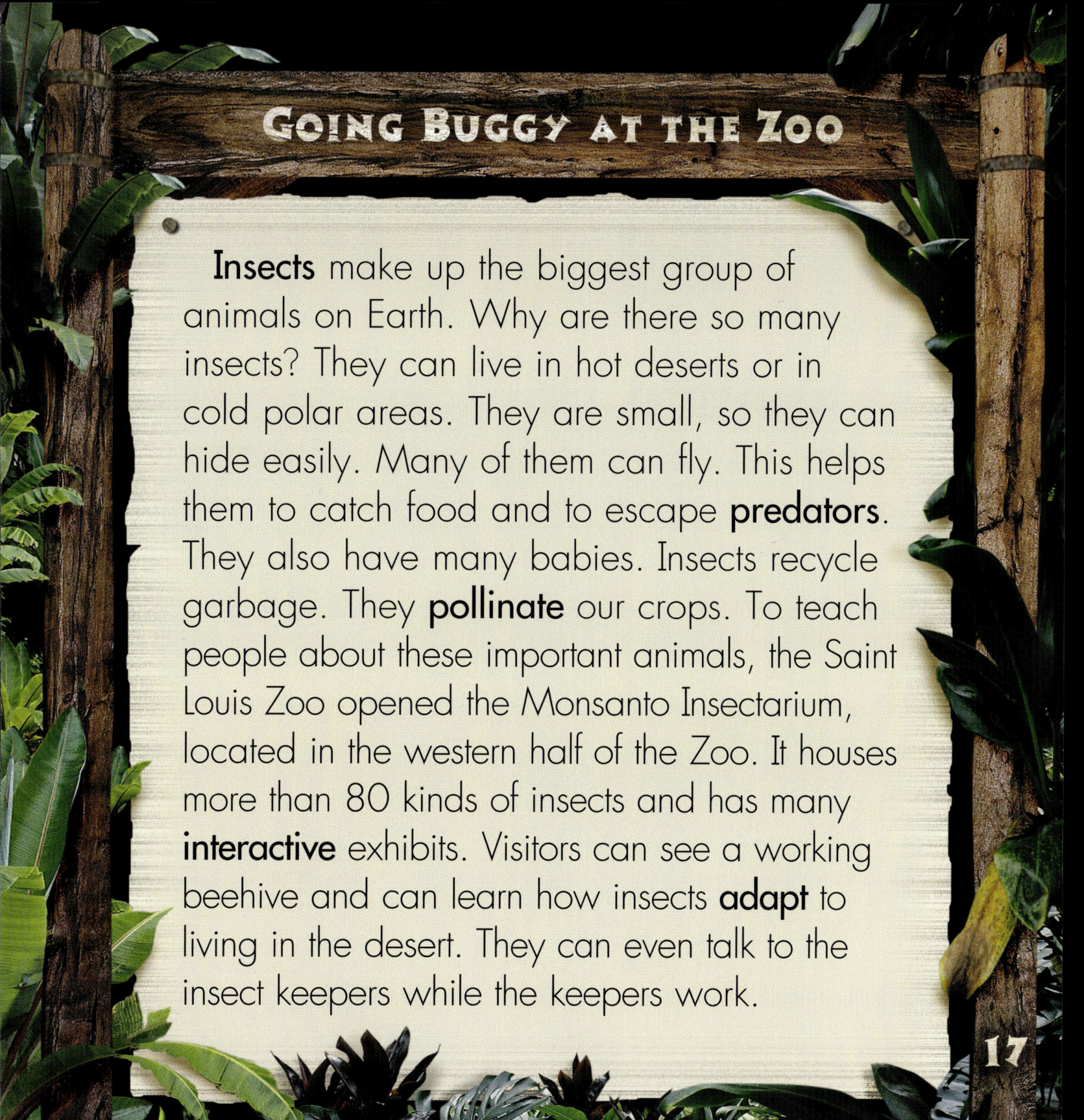

Insects make up the biggest group of animals on Earth. Why are there so many insects? They can live in hot deserts or in cold polar areas. They are small, so they can hide easily. Many of them can fly. This helps them to catch food and to escape **predators**. They also have many babies. Insects recycle garbage. They **pollinate** our crops. To teach people about these important animals, the Saint Louis Zoo opened the Monsanto Insectarium, located in the western half of the Zoo. It houses more than 80 kinds of insects and has many **interactive** exhibits. Visitors can see a working beehive and can learn how insects **adapt** to living in the desert. They can even talk to the insect keepers while the keepers work.

Baby Animals

About 450 babies are born at the Saint Louis Zoo every year. They range in size from a ⅛-inch-long (.3-cm-long) **millipede** to a 6-foot-tall (2-m-tall) giraffe. Saint Louis Zoo keepers used to raise most of the babies in a **nursery**. Today most Zoo babies are raised by their mothers. This is good news, because the babies grow up in family groups. They learn how to act around other animals. The females learn what to do when they have babies of their own. If a mother cannot take care of her baby, it is raised by keepers and put back with its family as soon as possible. Soon after a baby is born, Zoo **veterinarians** give it a checkup. They weigh it, listen to its heartbeat, and make sure it is healthy.

DID YOU KNOW?

Each year Saint Louis Zoo animals eat about 22 tons (20 t) of carrots and 13 tons (12 t) of bananas.

This lesser kudu mother watches for danger while her baby nurses, or drinks a meal of milk.

Zookeepers weigh a giraffe baby the day after it is born. Zoo staff do checkups on Zoo babies within the first 24 hours of the babies' births.

Leopard babies stay indoors with their mothers until they are about three months old.

DID YOU KNOW? To save the Puerto Rican crested toad, the Saint Louis Zoo and other zoos sent thousands of crested toad tadpoles to Puerto Rico to grow up in their native ponds.

When placed in birds' nests, these fake eggs send out special radio signals that tell scientists how warm the mother birds keep their eggs and how often they turn them.

The Zoo's veterinarian helps to examine a giant panda at a zoo in China. Giant pandas are one of the many types of endangered animals that the Saint Louis Zoo is working to save.

A Helping Hand

When animals are hunted or when their lands are changed by humans, the animals' populations become smaller. When their numbers are low, we say that animals are **endangered**. When there are no more animals of a certain **species** left, we say that species is **extinct**. The Saint Louis Zoo has 53 kinds of endangered animals. The Zoo works with other zoos to keep these animals from dying out.

To help the endangered ducks and geese that lay their eggs near the Zoo's lakes, Zoo scientists put special, fake eggs in the nests. These special eggs show the scientists how the mother birds care for their eggs. The scientists can then hatch the eggs in **incubators**, so more birds can be born in safety.

Beyond the Zoo

With more and more people living on Earth, there is less room for animals. People must have food and shelter. We farm, cut down trees, and burn fuels. These actions change our planet. We need to stop the bad changes. None of us can live if forests, animals, good soil, and fresh air are gone. The Saint Louis Zoo works with other groups to help the animals in zoos and those in the wild. The Web site www.beyondzoo.org explains some of the work zoos are doing. In one Saint Louis Zoo project, scientist Paule Gros is working with native peoples on the Bosawas **Reserve** in Nicaragua. Bosawas is home to many endangered animals. Gros is training native rangers to save the animals for the future.

Glossary

adapt (uh-DAPT) To change to fit into new conditions.
birds of prey (BURDZ UV PRAY) Birds that hunt live animals for food.
capybaras (ka-pee-BAR-uz) The largest rodents in the world.
destruction (dih-STRUK-shun) Breaking or destroying something.
endangered (en-DAYN-jerd) In danger of no longer existing.
exhibits (ig-ZIH-buhts) Displays designed for people to come and see.
extinct (ik-STINKT) No longer existing.
habitats (HA-bih-tats) Surroundings where an animal naturally lives.
incubators (ING-kyuh-bay-terz) Machines that keep eggs warm and safe so they can hatch.
insects (IN-sekts) Small animals with six legs, three body parts, two feelers, and no backbone.
interactive (in-ter-AK-tihv) Able to respond or to change when played with.
mesh (MEHSH) A stretchy, netlike fabric.
millipede (MIH-lih-peed) A flat, wormlike animal with many pairs of legs.
moat (MOHT) A deep waterway that people and animals cannot cross.
nursery (NURS-ree) A place where babies are cared for.
pollinate (PAH-lih-nayt) To carry pollen from one plant to another, which helps more plants to grow.
predators (PREH-duh-terz) Animals that kill other animals for food.
pygmy (PIHG-mee) Small, or smaller than the usual kind.
recycling (ree-SY-kling) Using things again instead of throwing them out.
reserve (rih-ZURV) A place where animals are safe.
species (SPEE-sheez) A single kind of plant or animal.
veterinarians (veh-tuh-ruh-NEHR-ee-unz) Doctors for animals.
volunteers (vah-luhn-TEERZ) Workers who help without pay.
wetlands (WEHT-landz) Shallow, marshy areas near rivers and oceans where many water creatures live.

23

Index

B
beehive, 17
birdcage, 5
birds of prey, 9
Bosawas Reserve, 22

C
capybaras, 10

E
Emerson Children's Zoo, 9
extinct, 21

F
Frog Surround, 9

G
Gros, Paule, 22

H
Hip Hop Swamp, 9

I
incubators, 21

L
Living World, 14
Lizzie, 14

M
Mississippi River, 5
Monsanto Insectarium, 17

P
Perkins, Marlin, 5
predators, 17

R
Raja, 13
River's Edge, 10, 13–14

V
veterinarians, 18
volunteers, 6

W
wetlands, 10, 14
Wild Kingdom, 5
World's Fair, 5

Web Sites

Due to the changing nature of Internet links, PowerKids Press has developed an online list of Web sites related to the subject of this book. This site is updated regularly. Please use this link to access the list:
www.powerkidslinks.com/gzus/stlouisz/